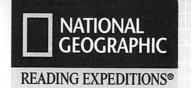
NATIONAL GEOGRAPHIC
READING EXPEDITIONS®

PLANET PATROL

Mountain Adventure

By Rebecca L. Johnson

Illustrated by Carol Heyer

T0308460

PICTURE CREDITS
6 left to right © blickwinkel/Alamy, © David Muench/Corbis; 64 © Gerry Ellis/Minden Pictures.

Produced through the worldwide resources of the National Geographic Society, John M. Fahey, Jr., President and Chief Executive Officer; Gilbert M. Grosvenor, Chairman of the Board; Nina D. Hoffman, Executive Vice President and President, Books and Education Publishing Group.

PREPARED BY NATIONAL GEOGRAPHIC SCHOOL PUBLISHING
Ericka Markman, Senior Vice President and President, Children's Books and Education Publishing Group; Steve Mico, Senior Vice President, Publisher, Editorial Director; Francis Downey, Executive Editor; Richard Easby, Editorial Manager; Bea Jackson, Director of Design; Cynthia Olson, Art Director; Margaret Sidlosky, Director of Illustrations; Matt Wascavage, Manager of Publishing Services; Lisa Pergolizzi, Sean Philpotts, Production Managers, Ted Tucker, Production Specialist.

MANUFACTURING AND QUALITY CONTROL
Christopher A. Liedel, Chief Financial Officer; Phillip L. Schlosser, Director; Clifton M. Brown III, Manager.

EDITORS
Barbara Seeber, Mary Anne Wengel

BOOK DEVELOPMENT
Morrison BookWorks LLC

BOOK DESIGN
Steven Curtis Design

ART DIRECTION
Dan Banks, Project Design Company

Published by the National Geographic Society
1145 17th Street, N.W.
Washington, D.C. 20036-4688

ISBN: 0-7922-5856-8
ISBN: 978-0-7922-5856-8

18 19 20
7 8 9 10
Printed in the United States of America

Contents

Destination: Wolf Country

Dr. Bender had just finished reading the last application. Hundreds had arrived in response to the advertisement he'd posted a month ago. Four applications stood out as the best. Dr. Bender sent an e-mail to Leroy, Traci, Tamara, and Jeremy. By tomorrow morning, they would know that they were going to the Rockies!

Leroy Patterson, age 13
Muncie, Indiana
I love science but hate being indoors. Being a field biologist, like Dr. Conner, is my idea of the perfect job.

Traci Kincaid, age 12
Sheridan, Wyoming
I want to be a wildlife photographer when I grow up. The chance to take pictures of wolves in the wild would be a dream come true.

Attention Young Explorers!

EcoAware is dedicated to promoting science and environmental awareness around the world. We want to involve young people in our research projects. EcoAware will give four students, ages 11 to 13, an opportunity to be interns with a wolf biologist, Dr. Joe Conner, in Idaho for one month. Dr. Conner monitors wolf packs that live in the wilderness areas of central Idaho. If you are interested, fill out the application below. Send it to Dr. Alan Bender at EcoAware.

Tamara Kulawea, age 13 Honolulu, Hawaii
I've seen nature programs on TV where scientists track animals with radio collars. I'd love to see how that works.

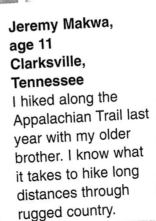

Jeremy Makwa, age 11 Clarksville, Tennessee
I hiked along the Appalachian Trail last year with my older brother. I know what it takes to hike long distances through rugged country.

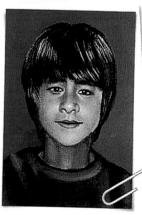

The Rocky Mountains

After the interns accepted their assignment, Dr. Bender e-mailed them this fact sheet about the Rocky Mountains.

THE ROCKY MOUNTAINS

The Rocky Mountains are located in western North America. The Rockies extend from Canada, in the north, to New Mexico, in the south.

The Northern Rockies stretch through the states of Idaho and Montana and north into Canada. They contain dense forests of evergreen trees. The forests are home to black bears, deer, elk, moose, and gray wolves.

The Gray Wolf almost became extinct in the Northern Rockies a hundred years ago. In the 1970s, gray wolves became protected animals. They were brought back, or reintroduced, into the northern Rockies and other parts of the country.

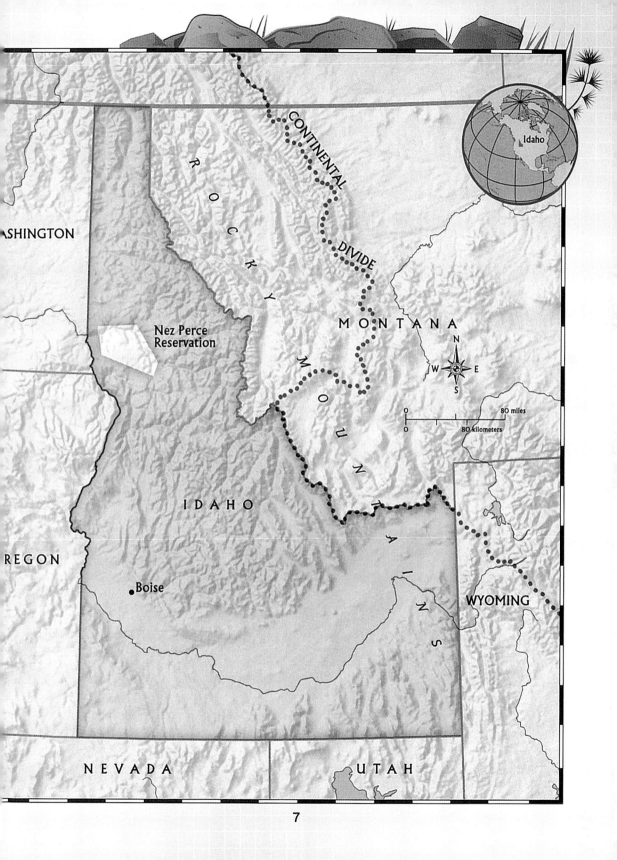

WASHINGTON

CONTINENTAL DIVIDE

ROCKY

Nez Perce
Reservation

MONTANA

IDAHO

M
O
U
N
T
A
I
N
S

Boise

OREGON

WYOMING

NEVADA

UTAH

Idaho

N
W E
S

80 miles
0
0
80 kilometers

CHAPTER 1

Into the Wilderness

Jeremy pressed his face against the window of the plane. Below were the rugged peaks of the Idaho Rockies. Some were capped with snow.

"I'll bet we're passing over the Continental Divide right now," Jeremy said to Traci, who was sitting next to him in Row 15.

"The Continental Divide? What's that?" asked Traci. She was busy putting fresh batteries in her digital camera.

"It's kind of like a dividing line," Jeremy replied. "It runs along the crest of the Rocky Mountains. Rivers on the west side of the Divide flow toward the Pacific Ocean. Rivers on the east side flow toward the Mississippi River."

"Awesome!" cried Traci. She flicked on her camera and leaned toward the window. "Maybe I can get a picture of it."

Leroy giggled from the row behind Traci and Jeremy. "The Continental Divide isn't something you can take a picture of, Traci," said Leroy, shaking his head.

"It's not like someone's drawn a line along the mountaintops, showing where it is," Tamara added. "You only know it's there by the direction that rivers flow down the mountain sides."

"Oh," Traci said, sounding disappointed. She sat back in her seat. "I'm just excited and I don't want to miss anything."

"That's the right attitude to have, Traci," said Dr. Bender from across the aisle. "Recording in pictures what you see and do is a great idea. But I want you all to record it in writing, too."

Dr. Bender pulled his briefcase out from under the seat in front of him.

"Here you go," he said. He handed each one of the interns a book. The books were all the same: dark green with the EcoAware logo on the cover.

Tamara flipped through her book. "But the pages are blank."

"It's up to you to fill them," Dr. Bender responded. "These are your official journals. The members of the EcoAware board and I want you to write down everything you see and do and learn while working with Dr. Conner. Keeping good records is a very important part of a scientist's job."

Dr. Bender continued. "You shouldn't have any trouble finding something to write about. You'll be helping Dr. Conner track radio-collared wolves through the forest. You'll be counting wolves in different wolf packs. You might see wolf pups, too. All of that information helps scientists figure out how large the wolf population is in central Idaho and how it's growing."

"I didn't know until I started reading about wolves that they were once common throughout the United States," remarked Tamara. "I thought they'd always been pretty rare."

"No, people **systematically** killed them," said Leroy. He took a pen out of his pocket. "They were almost wiped out." He opened his journal to the first page. "And I think that writing about this story is a good way to start my journal."

----

systematically – in a way that is thorough and regular

Endangered Wolves

by Leroy

Many European settlers who came to America were afraid of wolves. They saw them as a danger to people and livestock. In 1630, the Massachusetts Bay Colony offered rewards to people who killed wolves. The slaughter of wolves continued for the next three hundred years. It's estimated that 100,000 wolves were killed per year between 1870 and 1877. By the 1930s, gray wolves had been eliminated from most of the 48 states. Finally, in 1973, Congress passed the Endangered Species Act. After that, people began working to save wolves from extinction.

Jeremy was studying a map. "According to my calculations, we should be landing in Boise, Idaho, in about 15 minutes."

"I'll be ready," Traci said. She held up a small video camera. "I want to film our first meeting with Dr. Conner!"

"How many cameras did you bring?" Jeremy asked, raising an eyebrow.

"Five," she replied. "You never know what kind of camera you'll need for the perfect shot."

"Five?" Jeremy stammered. "Well, I know one thing. When we're tracking wolves through the forest with Dr. Conner, I'm never going to carry your backpack!"

As Jeremy predicted, the plane landed at the Boise airport less than 15 minutes later. Dr. Joe Conner was there to meet them. "Call me Joe," he said, shaking their hands. He wore weathered blue jeans, cowboy boots, and a felt hat with a broad brim. A braid of black hair hung halfway down his back.

Dr. Bender helped the interns carry their bags out to Dr. Conner's truck. Traci videotaped them loading all their gear. Then she asked everyone to pose for a group photo beside the truck. Jeremy sighed quietly and rolled his eyes.

"I'll see you in a month," Dr. Bender said, as Dr. Conner started the truck.

The scientist and the interns drove out of Boise. They headed into the mountains.

Joe tugged some papers out of the map pocket in his door. "Please pass these maps around to everyone, Tamara. I want to show you guys where we'll be. Right now, we're heading into the

Central Idaho Wolf Restoration Area," Joe said as the interns studied their maps. "You'll get to see a lot of it in the coming weeks. But we will be spending most of our time in the area I've circled in red."

Dr. Conner shifted into a lower gear. The road was getting steeper. Tall evergreen trees covered the rocky slopes that rose up beside the road.

Traci pulled out her video camera and aimed it out of the window. She videotaped the passing road and trees.

Leroy was still studying the map. "Hey Joe, when were wolves first **reintroduced** into this area?" he asked.

"In 1995, biologists working for the U.S. Fish and Wildlife Service captured

---

reintroduce – to place an animal that was once native to an area back into the area

some wolves in Canada," Joe explained. "They released 15 wolves into central Idaho that year and another 20 in 1996. Those wolves became the founders of all the wolf packs that are here now."

"How many wolves are there?" Tamara asked.

"Currently, there are more than 40 wolf packs in the restoration area," Joe replied. "When you add all of the wolves from each pack together, we've got about 450 wolves."

"Wow!" exclaimed Leroy. "You went from 35 wolves to 450 in about a dozen years!"

"Yes, the reintroduction has gone better than anyone expected," Joe said. He smiled. "The wolves like it here."

Traci put down her camera. "Do all the wolf biologists work for the Fish and Wildlife Service?" she asked Joe.

"Some work for Idaho's Department of Fish and Game," the scientist replied. "And others— like me—are Nez Perce."

Joe continued. "Like many other Native Americans, the Nez Perce have always felt a close connection to gray wolves. It seems only right that we're helping to manage their recovery, don't you think?"

Wolves and the Nez Perce

by Traci

The Nez Perce, or Nimi'ipuu as they call themselves, live on reservation lands in north-central Idaho. Wolves have long been important to their culture. Joe taught us the word for wolf in the Nez Perce language. It's He'me.

"Here's where we leave the pavement," Joe said, braking suddenly. He turned onto a narrow gravel road.

Most of the time, the interns could see only forest. But every now and then, they'd round a curve and suddenly be out in the open, hugging the side of the mountain. The ground seemed to fall away at the edge of the road, plunging down hundreds of feet into a deep green valley.

Up, up, up they drove. They crossed a small stream. The clear, cold water gurgled and splashed across their path. Then it slid over the edge of the road to become a roaring waterfall.

Just when it seemed like the ride would go on forever, the road opened up. Ahead was a small wooden building nestled among the trees.

"Welcome to the field station," Joe said, pulling up in front of the building.

A cool wind sighed through the tops of the pine trees overhead. The interns followed Joe up the path toward the building.

Their new home was simple and snug. There was a main room with a table, a sink, and a wood-burning stove. Two smaller rooms had bunk beds along the walls.

"You're all probably starting to get hungry. But how about a little hike before dinner?"

Traci nodded excitedly. "Let's explore first!" she said. "I'll just grab another camera." The other interns smiled as they exchanged glances.

From the back of the field station, a small trail led off into the trees. They followed it for a few minutes. Joe suddenly stopped.

"And what do you make of those?" he asked the interns. He pointed at some large paw prints in the damp ground.

"Are they wolf tracks?" Leroy asked in an excited whisper.

Joe nodded. "I'd say that the wolf that made them passed by only an hour or two ago."

Traci knelt down. She flipped up the flash on her camera. She took several close-up photos of

the wolf tracks. "Do you think the wolf is close by?" she asked.

"Hard to know," said Joe. "We'd have to track her—or him. We'll do that tomorrow. Right now, we're losing the light."

The sun had slipped behind the highest peak. Almost instantly, the air seemed cooler. The shadows deepened. Soon it would be dark.

On the way back to the field station, Joe suddenly stopped again. He put his finger to his lips. "Listen," he whispered.

From off in the distance came a yap-yap-yap sound—almost like a dog barking. Then the sound changed.

Oooooooooouuuuuwwww!

The single howl was joined by another, and another, and then another. The interns stood spellbound, listening to the strange chorus.

Somewhere out in the distance, a pack of wolves was howling.

The Wolf Pack

Early the next morning, Joe laid out several pieces of equipment on the table along with breakfast. The scientist told the interns what they'd be doing over the next several weeks.

"Dozens of wolves in the area are wearing **radio collars** around their necks," he said. He passed around a collar for the interns to see.

"Each collar sends out a slightly different signal," Joe continued. "We pick up the signals with our receiver." Joe laid his hand on the metal case of the receiver. "We follow the signal and track the wolf until we catch up to it."

Joe flipped on the receiver so they could hear the signal it was picking up from the collar.

---

radio collar – a collar that allows tracking by radio waves

"We try to have at least one collared wolf in every pack," the scientist said. "That way, we can track the entire pack. When we catch up to a pack, we count how many members there are. By adding up the number of wolves in each pack, we can estimate the size of the entire wolf population in the restoration area."

Attaching a Radio Collar   by Tamara

To attach a radio collar, biologists need to catch a wolf first. Sometimes they do that by shooting a wolf with a dart gun. The darts are filled with a drug that makes the wolf fall asleep. While the wolf sleeps, the biologists attach a collar. As soon as the collar is attached, the wolf is set free.

After breakfast, the interns gathered outside with their backpacks. Traci's backpack bulged more than the others. "My cameras," she said. "I've just got to have them." She was wearing one camera around her neck. There were four others in her pack.

Jeremy eyed the pack. He'd been on a lot of hikes. "You'll be sorry," he told Traci. She raised her eyebrows at him and shrugged. She swung the heavy pack onto her back.

"We're in the territory of a wolf pack with about ten members," Joe explained. "They were the wolves we heard howling last night."

A Wolf Pack's Territory
by Jeremy

Gray wolves usually live and hunt in a specific area; that's their territory. How big a territory is depends largely on how much food is available. Wolves hunt and eat mostly elk, deer, moose, and caribou. They can cover a lot of ground tracking their prey—as much as 30 miles a day!

"The alpha male in this pack is wearing a radio collar," Joe said. "I have already set the receiver for his frequency."

"The alpha wolves are the leaders of the pack, right?" Traci asked.

"That's right," Joe replied, cinching up his backpack. "A wolf pack is a family. It usually contains a pair of parent wolves—the alpha male and alpha female. The other wolves in the pack are the alphas' offspring. The alphas are in charge. The other wolves follow their lead."

"And only the alpha wolves have pups, right?" Jeremy asked.

Joe nodded. "Right again. The alpha male and alpha female typically mate for life. From late winter to late spring, the alpha female digs a den. She gives birth to her pups there—usually four to six." The scientist swung his pack onto his back. "This is pup season, by the way," he added with a grin.

"How big are the pups when they're born?" Tamara asked.

"Small enough to fit in your hand," Joe replied. "They're born with their eyes closed, so they are totally dependent on their mother. The other pack members bring the alpha female food while she stays with her pups. Later, they take care of the pups whenever the alpha female isn't around. When the pups are seven to eight months old, they start hunting with the pack."

Joe checked the signal on the receiver and headed into the forest. The interns followed.

Morning sunlight filtered down through the branches. Birds called and chipmunks chattered all around them. Joe pointed out three deer standing beneath a big fir tree.

The path became steeper and more difficult as they went on. There were fallen trees and big rocks to climb over. Traci quickly began panting under the weight of her heavy pack. She started falling behind.

"Gotta . . . stop . . . and rest . . . " she said finally. She was sweating while slumping against a tree. They all stopped.

Tamara frowned. "Traci, maybe next time you should consider bringing only one camera. You're really slowing us down."

"Getting photos is important!" Traci shot back.

"So is actually getting to see the wolves!" Jeremy said.

"OK, OK," said Joe, stepping in. "Everybody, relax. This is our first day of tracking. We all have a lot to learn."

Traci stood up. She tightened the straps on her pack. "I'm ready now. I just needed to catch my breath. I won't slow you down again."

They kept walking. Joe checked the receiver. "The signal's very strong now," he said softly. "We're close. No talking."

Farther up the slope, they came to a shallow **ravine.** Joe motioned for the interns to crouch down behind some rocks.

The interns pulled out their binoculars. They scanned the ravine and the slopes above it. The wolves were lying in the sun on a rock ledge halfway up the side of the ravine. Through binoculars, the interns could see the wolves clearly. They counted nine, including the alpha male. He was easy to spot with his radio collar.

The interns watched the wolves for several hours. The alpha male was constantly on the lookout for danger. He sniffed the air. His ears swiveled as he listened for anything out of place in the forest sounds. He watched over his pack like a protective father.

----
ravine – a narrow valley with steep sides

Writing in their EcoAware journals, the interns noted everything the wolves did. In hushed whispers, they asked Joe questions and he answered back softly. From behind a big boulder, Traci took a lot of photographs.

Wolf Communication
by Leroy

Wolves communicate their moods through their body language. The easiest ones to recognize are aggression, fear, and playfulness. When a wolf is showing aggression, it will stand up tall, hold its head high, and bare its teeth. The hair on its back stands straight up. The wolf will usually growl or bark.

A wolf that is frightened lowers its body, flattens its ears to its head, tucks its tail between its legs, and closes its mouth. It might roll over and show its belly.

When a wolf wants to play, it will do a play bow! It raises its rear end and lowers its front half to the ground. The wolf will sometimes bark once and wag its tail.

Finally, Joe signaled that they should pack up their things. Quietly, they crept away.

When they'd walked far enough from the wolf pack, Leroy asked a question. "Where was the alpha female? I didn't see her."

"I'd guess that she's holed up in a den with her pups," Joe replied. "Maybe sometime this month you'll get a chance to see them."

"I sure hope so," said Jeremy. He flipped through his journal. "Wow, I sure took a lot of notes today. I have at least seven full pages written. I can't believe how much we saw and did this morning."

The corners of Joe's mouth turned up slightly. "Oh, this is just the beginning. I'll be keeping all of you plenty busy."

The next five days flew by. Joe taught the interns to read wolf tracks like experts. They could tell if the wolf that made a set of tracks was walking, trotting, or running at full speed. "The farther apart the tracks are," Joe had told them, "the faster the wolf was moving at the time it made them."

Joe took the interns into a different part of the restoration area every day. They tracked down a dozen different radio-collared wolves. They located a dozen different packs.

The interns counted—and Traci photographed —every wolf they saw. With Joe's help, they created a map of the locations of the packs they'd seen. They compared their maps to official maps that showed the locations of every known wolf pack in the restoration area.

During this busy time, the interns also met and helped several other wolf scientists. They were very excited to ride in a helicopter with one. They helped her spot and count wolves from the air.

They helped another biologist capture a young wolf and put a radio collar on it. It was the first time they'd seen a wolf up close. The wolf had been shot with a dart gun. It was asleep while the scientist worked. The interns gently stroked the sleeping wolf's thick, gray fur.

"She looks a lot like a big dog," Tamara had said, studying the wolf's muzzle and pointed ears.

After the collar was on, they'd stayed until the wolf woke up. It blinked its eyes and stood up. The wolf took a few shaky steps. Then it bounded away into the woods.

Their sixth day at the field station was clear and bright. Joe wanted to check on the pack they'd seen on their first day in the field. "Maybe we'll

see the pups," he said. "It's about time for them to be coming out of the den."

Along the way, they spotted elk tracks in the damp ground. They also saw where a black bear had been munching on berries.

It was Leroy who spotted the wolf tracks. And something else.

Leroy touched a dark stain on the ground beside the tracks. He looked at his fingertips. They were red.

Joe examined the stains. "This is blood. The wolf that made these tracks is injured. It's not only bleeding. It's also walking very slowly. You

can tell by how close together the tracks are,"
he said pointing to them. "Let's try to find it."

Joe and the interns followed the tracks. There
were more drops of blood, closer together.

"Is that the wolf?" Traci asked softly. She
pointed to a gray shape ahead of them.

Joe approached the injured wolf cautiously. It
was lying on its side. Above its shoulder, the fur
was soaked with blood.

Joe called out. The wolf didn't move. He
crouched beside the body. With one hand he
reached out and touched the wolf's back feet.
The wolf still didn't move.

"Is he dead?" Tamara asked in a shaky voice.

Joe laid his head against the wolf's chest.
"No," he said, looking up. "He's still breathing.
His heart is still beating. But he's badly hurt."

The interns gathered around the injured wolf.
They stared at his bloody shoulder.

"Do you think he was in a fight with another
wolf?" Jeremy asked.

"No, I'm afraid not," Joe said, shaking his head
sadly. "This wolf has been shot."

Killer on the Loose

"Who would shoot a wolf?" Tamara asked, looking horrified.

Joe stood up. "A rancher, most likely. If a wolf attacks someone's sheep or cattle, that person has the right to kill the wolf."

"But I thought wolves were an endangered species," Jeremy said.

"They were, but they're doing very well. Their numbers have gone up so much that they have been downgraded to threatened status in Idaho," Joe replied. "But for the reintroduction program to be successful, people and wolves have to coexist. If wolves attack livestock, something must be done to stop them. Otherwise, we'll have a lot of angry people on our hands."

Joe slipped off his backpack. "The thing is, wolves seldom kill livestock. In a given year, many more sheep and cows die of disease, bad weather, and attacks from dogs than from attacks by wolves." He sighed. "But wolves are predators. And sometimes the chance for an easy meal is simply too good to pass up."

At-Risk Animals and Plants
by Traci

Last night Joe explained that biologists often talk about two major categories of at-risk animals and plants. An endangered species is an animal or plant that's in danger of dying out (going extinct) in most of the places it's found. A threatened species is an animal or plant that's likely to become endangered in the near future.

"So you think this wolf may have killed cattle or sheep?" Tamara asked. "And it was a rancher who shot him?"

"The only thing I know for sure," Joe replied, "is that we need to move fast if we want to save this wolf." The scientist pulled a small satellite phone out of his backpack. "I always carry this in case of an emergency," he said. He flicked the phone on. "We're going to need help getting this injured wolf out of here and down to a vet."

Leroy paced the room while Tamara, Traci, and Jeremy sat on the hard plastic chairs that lined the wall. The vet's office smelled like rubbing alcohol, dog food, and medicine.

A door opened. Joe came over to them. He look very relieved.

"Good news!" he said. "The wolf lost a lot of blood. But the vet said the bullet didn't do serious damage. She's sure he'll recover just fine. I have already reported the shooting to the wolf recovery program," Joe explained. "So now we wait and see if anyone admits to shooting a wolf."

A phone rang in another room. A moment later, the veterinarian's technician poked his head around the corner.

"Dr. Conner—phone call for you," he said, handing the scientist the phone.

"Conner here," Joe said. He listened closely. "I see. And when was this?" Joe pulled a pen out of his pocket. "Where's the ranch located?" He scribbled a note on a piece of paper.

Joe hung up. He handed the phone back to the technician and thanked him. "That was fast," he said, turning to the interns. "A rancher called the Fish and Wildlife Service a little while ago. He said he shot a wolf yesterday morning. He claims that it killed one of his sheep."

Joe picked up his hat. He slipped it onto his head. "Come on, kids," he said. "Let's go visit the scene of the crime."

Joe stopped the truck in front of the rancher's house. Behind it was a big green pasture where a herd of sheep grazed. Beyond the pasture stood the dark green forest.

Joe and the interns climbed down from the truck. They whirled around at the sound of a low, deep growl. A big dog with shaggy gray fur had silently come up behind them. The dog's lips were pulled back, revealing scary, pointed teeth.

"Nice doggie," said Leroy, trying to be calm.

At the sound of Leroy's voice, the dog leaped forward. It crouched directly in front of him, barking and snarling.

"Back, Rex, back!" a wiry man with steel-gray hair called out. He was striding across the yard toward them.

The dog suddenly stopped barking. But he kept growling at Joe and the interns.

"He won't hurt you, son," the man said briskly. "His bark is worse than his bite, as the saying goes." He pulled the dog away from Leroy. The dog snarled once more and fell silent.

Joe put out his hand. "I'm Dr. Joe Conner with the wolf recovery program. These young people are EcoAware interns working with me for the next few weeks. Are you Ed Gibson?"

"Yes, sir, I am," the rancher replied, briefly shaking the scientist's hand. He nodded his head curtly to the interns.

"I learned a few hours ago that you called in a report of a wolf attack," Joe said. "You said that one of your sheep was killed. And you shot the wolf that did it. Is that correct?"

"Darn wolves are a menace," Mr. Gibson replied angrily. "They're killers—every one of them. Reintroducing them around here was the worst idea anyone ever had."

"I'm sorry you feel that way," Joe replied. "We're trying to do our best to restore a threatened species. We try to protect the interests of people like you at the same time."

Wolves and Livestock   by Tamara

Not everyone likes the idea of having wolves for neighbors. That's especially true of ranchers. Wolves that kill sheep or cattle are a problem. To try to solve the problem, wolf biologists may capture a troublemaking wolf and release it in a remote part of the restoration area, far away from ranches. If that doesn't work, then the wolf may be humanely put to sleep. At first that seemed cruel to me. But Joe explained that some problem wolves have to be sacrificed so that the wolf population as a whole can survive.

"Well, then, you need to work harder," the rancher snapped, folding his arms across his chest. "Because of your wolves, another one of my sheep is dead."

Joe's eyebrows shot up. "Another one?"

Mr. Gibson nodded. "It's the third sheep I've lost this month. All were killed in exactly the same place, where my pasture runs close to the trees. They were killed the same way, too. The wolf tears the sheep's throat out, then takes off. It doesn't even eat them! All wolves are killers!"

Joe frowned. For a few seconds he said nothing. He seemed lost in thought. "What happened with this most recent killing?" Joe finally asked.

"Two nights ago, I heard a ruckus around 11 p.m.," Mr. Gibson began. "I grabbed my gun and headed to the pasture as fast as I could. But the wolf saw me coming. He turned and ran off into the forest before I could shoot him. I just caught a glimpse of him."

"So you didn't shoot the wolf right there and then?" Joe asked calmly.

"Nah, I waited until morning," the rancher answered. "When it was light, I went looking for tracks. There were tracks all around the dead sheep. I followed one clear set of tracks into the forest. I found that sheep-killing wolf an hour later. He was drinking from a stream, as nice as you please. So I shot him. I just wish I'd killed him."

Tamara knew she shouldn't interrupt, but she couldn't help herself. "But Mr. Gibson, how could you be sure that the wolf you shot was the one that killed your sheep?" she asked.

The rancher glared at her. "A wolf hanging around that close to my property? He's the one, all right. No doubt about it."

"Mr. Gibson, could we see where the attack occurred?" Joe asked politely.

"The sheep has already been carted off to the disposal plant," Mr. Gibson replied curtly. "But I'll show you where it all happened."

Joe took a step forward. A menacing snarl erupted from the rancher's dog.

"Rex! Quiet!" Mr. Gibson shouted. He turned sharply on his heel.

The ground where the sheep had been killed was all mud and torn-up grass. There were animal tracks everywhere.

Joe walked around, studying the ground. All the while, Mr. Gibson kept talking about how wolves were killers. And his dog kept growling.

Leroy, Tamara, and Jeremy followed Joe closely. Traci quickly fell behind, though. As usual, she had a camera in her hands. She was taking pictures of the muddy ground where the sheep had been killed.

Jeremy watched her for a moment, shaking his head. "That's all she ever does—take pictures," he murmured to Leroy.

Mr. Gibson showed Joe the wolf tracks he'd followed into the forest. "I think the tracks tell the story pretty well," the rancher said. "The wolf killed the sheep and then took off into the woods."

Traci photographed the tracks Mr. Gibson had pointed out. Then she moved closer to the woods, snapping photos as she went.

Joe straightened up. He nodded thoughtfully. Then he extended his hand to the rancher once more. "Thanks for letting us look around, Mr. Gibson," he said, shaking hands.

"I assume that since you've seen all of this, you'll make sure that wolf I shot is put down," the rancher said. "He's a killer for sure."

Joe adjusted his hat. "We have a little more investigating to do," he said. "But if it's clear that the injured wolf did indeed kill your sheep, we'll make sure he doesn't do it again."

Mr. Gibson frowned. "No doubt about it. That wolf is the animal responsible. And if I see any more wolves on my property, I'll shoot them, too!"

"We'll be in touch," Joe said. He turned to the interns. "Let's go, guys."

They headed back to the truck and climbed in—except for Traci. She was taking pictures in the muddy driveway.

"Come on, Traci!" Tamara called impatiently.

"Just a second!" Traci cried. She moved to another spot and took three more photos.

"Done!" she said, stepping up into the truck.

Joe started the truck. They drove slowly down the muddy driveway toward the main road.

"So . . . Joe . . . " Jeremy said, haltingly. "You're going to have to put that injured wolf to sleep, aren't you?"

Joe shook his head. "No, I don't think so."

"But if he killed Mr. Gibson's sheep . . . " Tamara began to say.

"I don't think that our wolf is the one that killed the sheep," Joe replied.

"Neither do I," Traci said from the back seat. She held up her camera triumphantly. "And I've got the evidence right here!"

Laying a Trap

"This will only take a few seconds," Traci said. She tapped a key on Joe's laptop. The pictures from her digital camera began to download onto the computer.

Joe and the other three interns stood behind her, watching the laptop screen. They'd come back to the field station directly after leaving Mr. Gibson's ranch.

"OK, here we go," Traci said. Several dozen pictures appeared on the screen. She selected one image and made it bigger.

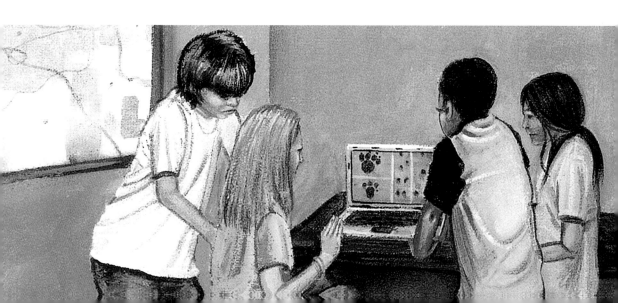

"This is a picture I took of the ground where the sheep was killed," Traci explained.

Leroy squinted at the image on the screen. "Whoa! Look at all those tracks! How are we going to make any sense of them?"

Joe leaned forward slightly, studying the photograph. "Well, when we were at the ranch," he began, "I noticed there were tracks from two different animals. I didn't have enough time to study them while we were there, but Traci's picture shows them really well."

"I noticed two sets of tracks, too," Traci replied. "That's why I started taking pictures. Look at this." She enlarged part of the image so they could see details.

Wolf Tracks
                                    by Jeremy
A wolf's foot is about four inches wide and five inches long. That makes a pretty big paw print, especially in soft or muddy ground. The biggest parts of the print are made by the toe pads. Above each of those is a small indentation. Those are made by the wolf's toenails!

"Hmmmm—these tracks on the left are definitely wolf prints," Joe said, pointing at the screen. "These tracks on the right are similar, but they're slightly smaller than wolf prints would be. And look at that," Joe said. "One of the toe pads is deformed."

The scientist stood up, looking thoughtful. "What we have here," he said, "are tracks made by two similar animals. One was a wolf. But the other one was a dog."

"Rex!" Jeremy blurted out.

"Yes, Rex," Traci said, nodding. She pulled up another photo and displayed it on the screen. "I took this picture by the truck, where Mr. Gibson had been standing with Rex."

The new photo showed a pair of boot prints. Beside them were paw prints made by Rex. One of the prints had a misshapen toe pad.

"They match!" Tamara said triumphantly. "Maybe Rex killed the sheep!"

"Hold on!" Leroy cried, shaking his head. "These pictures only prove that a wolf and Rex walked around in the mud where the sheep was killed. They don't prove which one of them killed the sheep."

Traci nodded in agreement. "Leroy's right. But these pictures," she went on, bringing up two more images, "tell a different story."

The first picture Traci showed them was of a line of wolf tracks, spaced fairly close together. They led from the fence at the edge of the pasture into the forest. The second photo showed another set of prints. They were definitely Rex's. The deformed toe pad was easy to pick out. Rex's prints also led from the pasture into the forest. But they were very widely spaced.

Joe's eyes widened. "Now *that's* interesting! You've got good eyes, Traci. I never spotted Rex's tracks heading into the forest when we were at the ranch."

The scientist turned to Leroy, Jeremy, and Tamara. "Come on—you're all good trackers. What do these tracks tell you?"

Leroy saw it instantly. "Hey! The wolf tracks are close together. That means he was walking away from the pasture. But Rex's tracks are far apart. He was running away at top speed!"

"And remember what Mr. Gibson said?" Tamara said excitedly. "He said the animal that killed his sheep ran off into the forest!"

Joe smiled, proud of his students. "Exactly. Based on these pictures, I'd say there's a good chance that it was Rex who killed the sheep and ran off when Mr. Gibson arrived. The wolf came along later. It probably smelled the dead sheep and was just checking it out. I wouldn't be surprised if Rex is responsible for Mr. Gibson's other dead sheep, as well."

Then the scientist's smile faded from his face. "Unfortunately, Traci, I don't think these pictures will be enough to convince Mr. Gibson."

"I know," Traci replied. "But I've got a plan to catch old Rex in the act!"

"Thank you very much, Mr. Gibson. We sure do appreciate it" Joe said into his cell phone before hanging up. He and the interns were back at the vet's office. They were excited to check on their injured wolf.

Joe turned to the interns. "Mr. Gibson said as long as we stay out of his pasture, he doesn't care what kind of equipment we set up on the other side of the fence."

A door opened across the waiting room. The vet Joe had spoken to the day before came over to greet them.

"Good news," she said, smiling. "Your wolf's wound is healing nicely. He's eating. His strength is coming back. I'd say he'll be ready to release in another three or four days."

"Can we see him?" Tamara asked.

The vet nodded. "Sure!"

She led them into a small, quiet, dimly lit room. The wolf was in a big cage along one wall. He

had a white bandage on his shoulder. He looked much better than when they had first found him.

The wolf raised his head and looked at them out of golden-brown eyes.

"He looks a lot better," Leroy whispered. Quietly, they backed out of the room. The interns thanked the vet. She smiled at them and waved good-bye. They followed Joe out of the clinic.

"Now all we need are some supplies," said Jeremy. He pulled the list they'd made earlier out of his pocket.

"Let's see—wire, electrical cord, sockets, light bulbs, a big battery . . . I think we can get it all at a hardware store," he said.

"All the ingredients we need," Traci said with a grin, "to lay our trap!"

Caught in the Act

Tamara twisted the last piece of wire. She gave the electrical cord a tug. It was nice and tight. She stood back and looked at the string of light bulbs. Twenty bulbs in a row were attached to the top strand of the barbed wire fence.

The spot where Mr. Gibson's sheep had been killed was just over the fence. Right now the herd was grazing about 20 feet away. Tamara could clearly see the sheep munching on grass.

Farther down the fence, Leroy and Jeremy attached the ends of the electrical cord to the big battery. "All set?" Jeremy called out to Tamara.

Tamara waved and nodded. "Give it a try!"

Jeremy threw the switch. The 20 light bulbs lit up.

"Perfect!" Traci called out. Tamara looked up into the tree where Traci and Joe were working. About 15 feet off the ground, they had built a platform of sturdy boards. Traci had her video camera already set up.

Traci adjusted the camera's focus. "The video camera is ready," she said. She motioned to Leroy and Jeremy. "Bring the battery up here. Then all we have to do is wait for dark to catch our killer in the act on video."

But catching the killer was harder than they'd thought. They sat huddled together on the platform in heavy coats, hats, and gloves. They sat in the chilly darkness, listening for the sounds of a sheep in distress. But all they heard was the hooting of owls and the squeaks of bats.

"Maybe this wasn't such a great idea," Leroy muttered, pulling the blanket he brought tighter around his shoulders.

"Patience, Leroy," Joe said softly. "That's something all good **field biologists** need. We just haven't been lucky yet."

The next night, their luck changed.

At sunset, the sheep had wandered close to the fence. As it grew darker, Joe and the interns lost sight of them. But an hour later the moon rose. The sheep were still there. In the moonlight, they looked like fuzzy gray patches against the blackness of the ground.

Around midnight, the sheep suddenly became alert. *Baa! Baaaa!* They milled around, turning this way and that. Their cries grew louder.

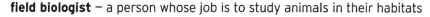

field biologist – a person whose job is to study animals in their habitats

"Look there!" Joe whispered, pointing out a dark shape. It was moving slowly along the inside of the fence.

The sheep began to run in circles. A low, rumbling growl came from the dark shape crouched near the fence. The animal was almost directly below their hideout in the tree.

The attacker made its move. Snarling, it leaped through the air toward the sheep.

"Lights!" Traci cried, turning on the camera. Leroy felt for the switch on the battery. He held his breath and flicked it on.

Suddenly, 20 lightbulbs blazed, lighting up the scene below. An animal with shaggy gray fur had just sunk its teeth into the shoulder of a young sheep. *Baaaaaa!* The sheep let out a terrified cry. With a growl, the furry attacker knocked the sheep to the ground. Jaws snapping, it moved in for the kill.

"Ready? Go!" Joe cried. They all began shouting at the tops of their lungs. Leroy and Tamara threw stones.

Startled, the furry predator let go of its prey. It looked up toward the shouting. Traci smiled as she zoomed the camera in on Rex's face. She kept

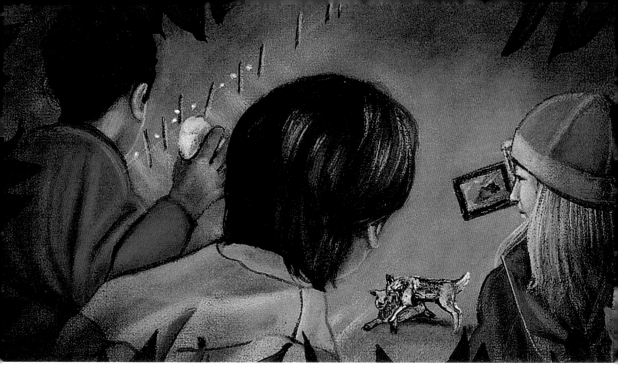

running the video camera as the dog raced off into the darkness.

The next day, Mr. Gibson was standing in the driveway as they pulled up. Rex stood beside him as Joe and the interns walked up to him.

"I had another wolf attack last night," Mr. Gibson said angrily. "I'll have you know that I almost lost another sheep."

"The wolf you shot is still recovering from its wounds at the vet's office," Joe said. "It couldn't have been the attacker."

"Must have been another wolf then," the rancher replied shortly. "Just proves my point. They're all killers."

"As it turns out," Joe said calmly, "we were on the other side of the fence last night. We scared off the animal that attacked your sheep—and we caught it on film. Would you like to see it?"

Mr. Gibson frowned. "I've seen plenty of pictures of wolves."

"But this one might surprise you," Joe responded. He motioned to Traci.

Traci stepped up to Mr. Gibson with her video camera. Rex growled at her. "Quiet, boy!" Mr. Gibson commanded.

Traci hit the play button on her camera. Mr. Gibson peered at the screen. His eyes narrowed as he watched the beginning of the attack. He was about to say something when Rex's face filled the screen. A look of amazement—and shock—washed over the rancher's face.

"Rex?" the rancher stammered, looking from the camera screen to his dog. "It can't be!"

"We caught him red-handed, Mr. Gibson," Joe said kindly. "We also have pictures of his tracks leading off from the last kill into the forest."

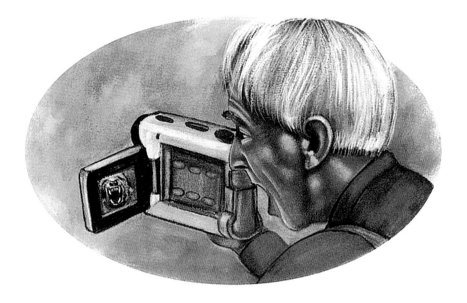

"What about the wolf tracks?" the rancher shot back. He was very upset.

"A wolf did arrive on the scene," Joe explained. "But he came after the attack, after you'd scared Rex off."

Mr. Gibson said nothing. He looked at Rex and then up at the pasture where his sheep were.

Then he turned back to Joe and the interns. He cleared his throat.

"I can't believe my own dog kills sheep," the rancher said "But I can't deny your pictures. Now that I think about it, Rex was always missing when those attacks occurred. I guess I just never put two and two together."

Mr. Gibson stared at the ground. "Well, I'll tell you the truth. I don't like having wolves around and I don't like having to admit that I was wrong, either." He looked up at the interns and Joe. "But it appears that I was wrong about the wolf. And I am sorry."

He turned toward his dog. "And from now on, Rex will be locked in the barn at night."

"Ready? One—two—three—LIFT!" Five pairs of hands lifted the cage out of the back of the truck. Joe and the interns carried it down the ramp. They set it on the ground.

The wolf blinked in the bright light. His bandages were gone. The healing wound showed in the shaved patch on his shoulder.

"So which one of you wants to open the cage door?" Joe asked, smiling.

Jeremy stepped forward. "I think Traci should get to do it."

Traci stared at him, surprised.

Jeremy went on. "We've all teased you about always taking pictures, Traci. But it was because of your pictures that we solved the mystery of Mr. Gibson's sheep attacks."

"And maybe convinced him to think twice before he tries to kill another wolf," Leroy added.

"Yes," Tamara said, nodding. "I think Traci should be the one to free our wolf."

Somewhat embarrassed, Traci smiled. "I'd be honored, guys. Thanks!"

Joe and the others watched as Traci released the catch on the door and slowly opened it.

The wolf pricked up his ears. He eyed the open cage door and the forest beyond it. He took a step forward. He sniffed the air. Then, with a quick glance back at Joe and the interns, he bounded out of the cage. Just a flash of gray fur, he disappeared among the trees.

"Do you think he'll find his pack again?" Tamara asked Joe.

"I'm not sure he has one," the scientist replied. "He seems to be a young wolf on his own. He probably left the pack he was born into a short while ago. Now he's looking for a mate and a new territory for his own pack."

"What if other packs don't like having a new pack around?" Jeremy asked.

"If they feel like they're being invaded, wolves aggressively defend their territories," replied Joe. "But, given time, the existing packs will learn to live with new neighbors."

"Like Mr. Gibson?" Traci asked, grinning.

"I think Mr. Gibson learned a lesson," Joe replied. "A lot of people don't understand wolves. When they learn more, they usually discover that wolves deserve a place in the wild."

Dispersing
                                            by Leroy
Many wolves leave their family pack when they're one to two years old. Biologists call this behavior "dispersing." Dispersing wolves travel around in search of a mate (another dispersing wolf of the opposite sex). Together, this new pair may start a pack in a territory of their own.

"I think we should write an article about our experience with Mr. Gibson, Rex, and the wolf," Tamara said suddenly. "If we got it published in a magazine, a lot of people would read it. Maybe it would change the way they think about wolves."

"Great idea!" cried Traci. She pulled a camera out of her sweatshirt pocket. "But we'll need photos of our group for the article. Everyone stand by the cage and squeeze together."

Traci squinted through the viewfinder. "OK, I want big smiles. Everybody say . . . "

At that moment, a familiar sound echoed through the trees—the howl of a wolf.

" . . . live free!" Traci finished.

"Live free!" Joe and the other interns shouted, grinning. As she snapped the photo, Traci hoped the wolf heard them.

Report to Dr. Bender

Imagine that Dr. Bender has asked you to write a one-page report about what you have learned about the environment and animals of the Rocky Mountains.

- Draw a cause-and-effect chart like the one below.

- Think about the causes and effects in the story. A cause is the reason something happens. An effect is the result, or what happens next.

- Look at the chart below for a sample.

- Fill in your chart with causes and effects that have to do with the environment and animals of the Rocky Mountains.

- Write a one-page report in which you explain two of the cause-and-effect relationships from your chart.

CAUSE	EFFECT
1. People passed laws to protect gray wolves.	1. The gray wolf population can now grow.

Read More About the Rocky Mountains

Find and read more books about the Rocky Mountains. As you read, think about these questions.

• What is the climate like in the Rocky Mountains?

• What types of wildlife are found in the Rocky Mountains?

• Why do scientists study the plants and animals of the Rocky Mountains?

• What have scientists learned from their studies in the Rocky Mountains?

SUGGESTED READING
Reading Expeditions
Science Issues Today:
Endangered Species

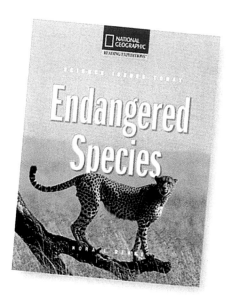